The Urban Educator's Survival Guide:
7 Proven Strategies From a Successful School Teacher's Classroom

Dennis Nappi II

Published by Service of Change, LLC
© 2014 Service of Change, LLC

All Rights Reserved. No part of this book may be reproduced, scanned, or distributed in any printed or electronic form without permission from the publisher.

ISBN: 978 0 9911375 2 7

For additional FREE resources, please visit

www.ServiceOfChange.com/Teachers

Contents

Arrange Your Room for Combat

Teaching Procedures

Get to Know Your Students

Journals

Classroom Kung Fu

Plan B, C, and D

Unplug

Final Thoughts

Additional Resources

Contacting the Author

Introduction

Whether you are a first year teacher, a seasoned veteran, or a current student preparing for your future career, this guide is designed to help *you!* As a teacher, I have worked in some of the most challenging districts, schools, and classrooms in the state of Pennsylvania. As I mentioned in my book, *Service*, I was trained as a soldier, special agent, and police officer before I became a teacher, and despite the many challenges I faced throughout my eleven-year military and law enforcement careers, teaching was the hardest thing I ever did.

I have worked in classrooms where my students were violent. I have encountered administrators who refused to support me. I have faced the challenges of working without adequate materials and I have dealt with the many frustrations that surround our current standardized-testing infestation. However, despite these challenges, I have found success with my students. It is because of my students that I have created this guide because I have witnessed just how desperately they need our help.

If you've ever read my blog or memoir, it's no secret that I am an advocate for education reform. I want to see a love for learning returned to all of our students, regardless of the economic status of their district. I know it's possible because I have witnessed some of the most difficult students grow to love learning after months of total defiance. With this guide you will be given some of the tools you need to lay the foundation to support challenging students and nurture a love for learning in your own classroom.

Change, however, especially in regards to education reform, cannot be done overnight and it cannot be done by one person alone. We need teachers, and we need teachers who care, to bring about that change. Change will take place in the classroom, on the front lines with students, and not through board meetings, political agendas, or data driven testing objectives. It is through the day-to-day interactions between teachers and students that the impact is made. Unfortunately, in classrooms with the greatest need there is often the greatest lack of support, resources, and compassion. This is where I hold the majority of my teaching experience. It is through my experiences in these classrooms, along with my experiences as a soldier and police officer, that I have compiled this guide. Everything I offer here has been successfully implemented in my classrooms and worked well with even the most challenging students. As you'll soon find out, this guide is comprised of 7 proven strategies that together, work as a system to balance the chaos of even the most challenging classrooms.

As a teacher, I'd like to personally thank you for taking on such a challenging and noble career. Our students are our future, and without caring and talented teachers like you to guide them, the world can become a very scary place. Education reform is possible, but can only come about through your efforts. I hope you find this guide helpful, and wish you all the best in your teaching career.

Strategy 1:
Arrange Your Room for Combat

They layout of your classroom is an essential yet often forgotten aspect of teaching. A good layout and distribution of resources supports learning and classroom management in a countless number of ways. However, it is not until we encounter a poor layout that we realize just how important this strategy is.

In any given class, a teacher is constantly assaulted with a barrage of requests and needs by students. If one hasn't properly prepared for this assault, teachers will quickly realize that an entire class can be wasted by simply trying to address dozens of minor needs and requests.

I always spend the beginning of my school year visualizing a typical class and trying to anticipate every possible disruption my students will throw at me. I find that the first few teacher days, before students return to school, are perfect for this. During that first teacher day, I evaluate these possible engagements and ask myself if a simple tactical arrangement of my room can avoid those disruptions. If the answer is yes, I incorporate it into my room layout.

Here is a basic example: A teacher is giving a lecture about the story the class is reading. Once the lecture is over, the teacher wants to transition to a guided writing assignment and instructs the students to take out their pencils and a piece of paper. Now, despite daily reminders, rewards, and reprimands about being prepared for class, there will *always* be students who come to class without the supplies they need. During my first year in an urban school, I was afraid my supplies would be stolen or damaged so I kept everything locked in a cabinet. When a student would ask me for a pencil or paper, I'd have to stop my instruction, take out my keys, walk to the cabinet, unlock the cabinet, take out the pencil, lock the cabinet, walk it over to the student, and then return to my position in the front of the room. This process generally took one to two minutes, which can be an eternity in a class with limited attention spans and interest! During the time it took me to get that single pencil, two students started talking, one started texting, three started drawing, and one fell asleep. I then needed to spend another one to three minutes getting these students back on task *and* I needed to reengage my entire classroom and re-stimulate their interest in the assignment. So from a simple request for a pencil, a teacher can lose almost 10 minutes of instruction time which could be almost 25% of the entire class period! In addition, I can almost guarantee that the instant you get the class back on task, another student will raise his hand and ask: *"Can I have a pencil?"* You then must repeat the process and at this point you have potentially lost half of your instruction time and the attention of your entire class.

So how can this be avoided? It's simple, and I am sure you have already figured it out. Keep your pencils out in the open, in a place that is easily accessible, *and* make sure they are already sharpened (which is a great task for a student who may need a temporary distraction). This way, when a student needs a pencil the burden and effort is on the student, leaving you free to continue instruction and keep the rest of the class engaged. Just be sure to place the pencils (and other supplies) in a "neutral zone," a place that will not generate distractions or disruptions for the one student or entire class. I often set up a table off to the side with extra paper, a stapler, pencils, a sharpener, and any other materials my students may need that day. In addition, be sure to establish a set procedure for when and how a student may obtain supplies from the table. (We'll discuss the importance of procedures in the next chapter).

Some other things to consider in the tactical arrangement of your classroom:

- *The arrangement of student desks. Will they promote disruptions or support learning?*
- *Location of text books (if students leave them in the classroom). Are they easily accessible?*
- *Access to your classroom phone – can you get to it quickly in an emergency or do you need to hurdle desks, students, and tables to reach it?*
- *The location of your teacher desk: If you are seated at your desk, can you see all of your students? Can you see the door so nobody enters or exits without you realizing it?*
- *Your personal belongings: Do you have a place to safely keep them to prevent theft or vandalism?*
- *Chalk, markers, & erasers: Do you have to go searching for them or are they easily accessible?*

The above-list is not all inclusive, and every single classroom will be different. But it is a great starting point. You will probably never be able to anticipate every single disruption, but designing a tactical layout for your classroom is an excellent preventative measure that can end up saving you *hours* of instructional time throughout the year. In the next section, we will discuss the importance of procedures and how they will nicely compliment your tactical layout.

Strategy 2:
Teaching Procedures

When I was in grad school, a professor once discussed the value of teaching classroom procedures. He said that if my students knew what to do (by following procedures), they would be able to direct more of their focus toward the learning process. As a police officer, my defensive tactics instructor taught me that "in a crisis, you resort to your highest level of training," because you don't often have time to think about what you are doing when facing a crisis. The beginning of a class can often resemble the chaos of a crisis situation with students scrambling in from the hallway filled with the wonderful distractions of friends, headphones, and cell phones. As I mentioned in the previous chapter, it's important to have a tactical layout in your classroom so your students can have access to their needed resources without wasting instruction time. But how should they access those resources? What steps do they need to take from entering your classroom, to obtaining those resources, to getting to their seats without incident or disruption? Without a procedure in place, the teacher could find a large group of students socializing at the supply table during the first ten minutes of class with no easy way to redirect them back to their seats quietly. This wastes time and leaves the classroom vulnerable for confrontations, distractions, and defiance.

With procedures in place, however, this situation would not arise, and if it does, the teacher will already have a set procedure on how to address it. Procedures hold both students and teachers accountable by providing a structure and flow to the classroom. They define both student and teacher roles and responsibilities, preventing the need for off topic questions and conversations. Normally, I spend my entire first month teaching procedures and I reinforce them as needed throughout the entire school year. Although I cover the required academic materials, I am always sure to incorporate the teaching of procedures and the reinforcement of those procedures, into my daily lessons during that first month.

The first week of school is the most important week in the entire school year. It is when teachers set the standards for their classrooms and show their students that they are prepared (because they care) to teach them and meet their needs. But how does a teacher demonstrate that level of preparedness? Handing students a syllabus shows them you plan on giving them a lot of work. Reading them a list of rules tells them you expect them to behave. But how can you demonstrate your expectations, enforce your rules, and ensure everything runs smoothly? By teaching them *how* to meet those expectations and modeling what they look like.

Here is an example of one of my favorite procedures, which actually incorporates several other smaller procedures. As I'll explain in a later chapter, journaling is an excellent strategy in itself, and I have developed a procedure to support this strategy. On the first day of school, I explain to my students that every single class will begin with a 5 – 10 minute journal writing activity. I point to my board and show them exactly where the prompt will be written and I give them the following instructions orally and in writing:

1. *When you come in the room, take out your journal (which is sometimes stored in the classroom) and a pencil (borrow one from the supply table if needed)*
2. *As soon as class starts, place your name on the top line on the left side and the date on the right (mm/dd/yy).*
3. *Skip one line*
4. *Copy the title of the journal, centered, on the next line*

5. *Skip one line*
6. *Copy the writing prompt from the board*
7. *Skip two lines*
8. *Answer the writing prompt in at least five sentences*
9. *If you finish before the time is up, free write until the time is up*

I provide my students with a sample journal page so they can see exactly what it looks like and I have them practice retrieving their journals and getting their page set up. I then inform them (with lots of praise for their efforts), that they are to follow this procedure every single day. I walk them through each and every step as a group. By explaining each step, it establishes my authority as a teacher, and it also allows them an opportunity to find success in their first assignment, helping to build self-esteem.

My students learn from the very first day of school that my expectation of them is to be seated in their desks writing in their journals by the time class starts. They also know that they can expect me to already have the journal entry on the board and to have pencils and paper available should they be unprepared that day. This helps build trust between the students and the teacher.

During that first week, I may spend 15 – 20 minutes at the beginning of each class on journals because I want to reinforce the proper procedure and the importance of following that procedure. When I grade the journals, I focus less on grammar and content and more on procedure and format. I may take a point off if they forget to skip a line, fail to put the date in the right spot, or only provide their first name. If things are a total disaster I may even have the entire class start over again by having them put back their journals, return to their seats, and then begin again as if they just arrived. Normally by the second week of school, they are coming in, getting their journals, and begin writing silently without any instruction from me.

By teaching this procedure, the tone is set for the function of your classroom. I often build off of this procedure and use it as a foundation for the other procedures I teach.

Some important procedures to consider in your classroom are:

- *Entering the classroom*
- *Using the restroom*
- *Getting supplies or books*
- *Sharpening pencils*
- *Fire & Emergency drills*
- *Going to the office or nurse*
- *Early dismissal*
- *What to do if a fight breaks out*
- *What to do if a student finishes all of his or her work early*
- *Packing up at the end of the class*
- *Cleaning up the classroom*
- *Leaving the classroom at the conclusion of class*

Once you start teaching procedures you will find that your instruction flows much smoother. Although you may focus less on content during the first few weeks of school, the time you will save throughout the course of the year will allow you extra hours of valuable, uninterrupted instructional time with your students.

Strategy 3:
Get to Know Your Students

My greatest strength as a teacher has been my ability to build relationships with my students. When I first started teaching, however, I lacked any real education or training as an educator. My undergraduate studies were in Criminal Justice and Spanish and all of my professional experience was in the fields of intelligence and law enforcement.

As a counterintelligence special agent, one of my main functions was to build relationships with the people I encountered. In order to protect the lives of American soldiers, I needed to identify people capable and willing to provide me with information about the enemy. I needed to recruit people to spy. I couldn't do this, however, if I wasn't capable of building and maintaining relationships. I needed people to earn my trust because I then needed to be able to convince them to do things that could put their lives or the lives of their loved ones in jeopardy.

In the classroom, I found that although lives weren't (usually) in jeopardy, my students often felt threatened when I would ask them to do something. My questions of: "Who threw the pencil," or "Where is Tyron?" often went unanswered because of the *snitches get stitches* mentality. When I'd ask a student to take out a book or complete a worksheet, they'd react as if I'd asked them to jump out the window or rob a bank.

I have often found that if a student doesn't have any connection to you, it is easier for them to try to hurt, offend, or disrupt you. They are not invested in you and see no need to show you respect. This mindset, unfortunately, can turn a simple lesson into a disaster. I realized that in order to teach my students, my students need to trust me. In order for my students to trust me, they need to get to know me. In order for them to get to know me, I need to get to know them. Since most of my students won't respect me or do any work for me unless they trust me, I begin this process on the first day of school. From the minute my students approach my classroom, I start building relationships. Before they enter my class, I stand in the hallway to greet them. I smile, shake hands, and if I know their name, greet them by name.

During the first week of school, I hand out a questionnaire asking students to tell me a little about themselves: hobbies, interests, favorite movie, etc. I give them some time to complete the assignment and then hold a discussion period to review their answers. Almost every time, I find that nobody wants to share anything about themselves and my requests for someone to tell me their favorite movie leaves a room full of silent, blank stares. To combat this, I complete the same form. I have realized that in order to build trust and ask students to share personal information with a stranger, then I should be doing the same. Now, instead of asking for students to tell me their favorite movie, I start off by telling them my favorite movie. I give several details about why I like the movie, sometimes throwing in other aspects of my life: "I like this movie because it reminds me of my Army training." Students then usually start asking me questions about myself, which I gladly share with them. After answering their question, however, I follow up with a question about themselves. Since the student has already invested in the conversation (and in me) nine times out of ten, the student will provide me with an honest answer and before we know it, the entire class is involved in a discussion. I have found this strategy works so well that there have been years when we could only review one question per day because everyone was so eager to contribute to the conversation. The students often think they are getting me to tell them a ton of information about myself and keeping us off topic. In reality, they are following my plan to get to know them in the specific amount of time I allotted for this essential activity.

It takes more than a knowledge of likes and dislikes, however, to build a relationship of trust between teacher and students. Students need to feel safe in your classroom; safe from violence, ridicule, and embarrassment. Students need to know that no matter what happens, you will always support them. I have found, as a special-education teacher, most of my students have given up on education and on teachers because they have been dumped in the special-ed room and forgotten about. If I want my students to trust me and do well, I need to prove to them that my classroom is safe for them to take educational risks. But how does one demonstrate this? Saying it isn't enough. A teacher must demonstrate this through actions, reactions, and interactions.

Here is an example: When reading *Red Riding Hood*, I may ask the question: "What happened to Red Riding Hood's grandmother?" A student may respond: "She turned into the wolf." Although the answer is incorrect, I take this opportunity to let my student know it is okay to make a mistake. "Are you sure?" I'll ask, giving them an opportunity to correct themselves. If they then realize that Grandma was eaten by the wolf, I praise them for the correct answer. If they still can't determine exactly what happened to her, I'll ask: "Can anybody help her out?"

Once the correct answer is provided, I will immediately return to the first student and praise her efforts: "That was a really good try. I can see how it can be confusing and you could easily conclude that she turned into the wolf. I actually think a werewolf twist would make an excellent rewrite! But do you understand now that she was eaten?" I'll have that student then find the passage that best explains the answer and praise her for her efforts. This positive approach helps students feel safe to take risks and learn to accept their own mistakes not as failures but as learning opportunities.

In order to continue to build positive and trusting relationships, it may be beneficial to follow these guidelines:

- *Stay positive – always find something positive to say, even when being critical*
- *Listen to your students – if they address a concern or share something personal, pay attention and give feedback (when appropriate)*
- *Be honest – don't be afraid to share personal experiences. Students want to know who you are, and telling them about yourself shows your trust in them.*
- *Set boundaries – Certain topics are off limits! There are things students don't need to know*

about you and things you don't need to know about them. Be clear about your boundaries, which will also help establish/maintain your role as an authority.

- *Start fresh – after an incident happens that requires a negative consequence, remind the student that the incident is in the past and tomorrow is a new day with a clean slate.*

Activities that can promote and foster a positive, professional relationship between teachers and students:

- *Journal writing*
- *Class discussions*
- *Two truths and a lie – tell the class two things that are true about you and one lie and have them determine the lie. They then have to do the same.*
- *Positive feedback/reinforcement*
- *Attending a student's sporting event or extra-curricular activity*
- *Following through with any promises you make*

Once you get to know your students, you will be able to recognize their moods which can be the difference between a major crisis and a successful lesson. For example, if a student comes in seeming down or angry, if you have a trusting relationship you can comfortably and privately ask the student what is wrong. The student may tell you, or may tell you to go away. If they tell you, you can then try to remedy the problem yourself or call in a guidance counselor to work with the student. If they refuse to speak with you, try telling the student: "Okay, everyone has a bad day. Just sit quietly over here and we can get caught up later. If you want to talk, my door is always open. If you don't want to talk to me, I can get you in touch with someone you're more comfortable talking to." You are then free to continue with your lesson. I have found that in many cases, within 10 minutes the student either reengages in the lesson or asks to go speak with a counselor. Either way, a potential crisis has been averted, learning continues in your class, and your distraught student gets the time or the attention he needs because you took the time to build trusting relationships with your students.

Strategy 4:
Journals

As I stated in the previous chapter, it is extremely important to get to know your students and in an earlier chapter, I also discussed the importance of establishing routines and procedures. Through my experience, I have found that journaling can provide a teacher with both an opportunity to get to know your students and is a great way to start establishing your classroom procedures.

Since my first year as a teacher, I have started every class with a journal entry. I have found journaling to be a great warm up activity for students that fosters independence and creativity. It gives students an opportunity to have an opinion and a voice and I found it is a great way to ease into a specific lesson or start the class. In addition, it helps improve their written expression!

As outlined in the procedures chapter, my students come in each day and gather their required materials. They always find a journal prompt written on the board, and get started right away. Once the bell rings and class has begun, I give them five minutes to write. I always give two and one minute warnings before their time expires so they are prepared to stop when I tell them.

Once they are finished writing, I ask if anyone is interested in sharing. This is one of the most important aspects of the assignment. In the beginning of the year, I may get one or two students and sometimes I even have to coax them to share. I often have at least one student every year who comes in and tells me that sharing "isn't his thing." I explain that I will not force anyone to share, and am just genuinely curious to hear their opinions. I then use the sharing period to listen to what my students have to say and I always ask follow up questions, point out the strengths of their writing, and offer constructive criticism on how to improve their writing. Once they are done sharing, I then share my response to model proper writing and discussion for my students.

The feedback I offer my students may sound something like this:

- *"How did that make you feel?"*
- *"That is exactly what I was looking for. Thank you for being so honest in your writing."*
- *"Your structure was great! You had an introductory sentence with three supporting details and a concluding sentence. Great job!"*

- *"You make a great point. I like the way you included these two facts. For your next entry, you may want to try adding a concluding sentence to complete your argument, but great job and thanks for sharing."*

I have found that my biggest challenge with journaling is limiting our discussion time and moving onto the next lesson. I always try to pick topics that may interest the students to include: school events, events in the news, parents, teachers, and philosophical questions like: *What would the world be like without money?* My students and I usually become so engaged in the conversation that we can easily lose track of time if I'm not paying attention. There have been times when the discussion has been so intense (and important) that I allowed it to continue for the entire class with an understanding that the next day we would work twice as hard to get caught up (and we did!)

Through journaling, I have learned so much about my students. They have opened up to me and told me some incredibly personal stories. We have had discussions about the death of family members and friends, drug use, and racial and cultural issues. As a white teacher in often predominantly black classrooms, journaling has provided an excellent opportunity for me to learn about a culture I previously knew very little about. It created a safe forum for open and honest discussions about multiple cultures and allowed us to explore racism and stereotypes in an educational fashion. As a teacher, these discussions have allowed for my greatest opportunities to learn about my students, their cultures, and how best to engage a wide variety of students with various strengths, weaknesses, and personality traits. In addition, it has reinforced in my students appropriate ways to engage in a mature, professional discussion or debate and show respect for differing opinions and ideas.

Regardless of which subject you teach, journaling can be the keystone that supports the entire foundation of your classroom. It provides structure, an opportunity to get to know your students, and opens up very engaging and educational discussions which can also be used as teachable moments. Social Studies, Science, Health, and even Math can all start with a 5 minute journal entry about course-specific topics. I promise that if you implement this activity with the intent of getting to learn more about your students, you will find the process very rewarding and successful.

Strategy 5:
Classroom Kung Fu

Teaching should be chaotic. Students should be challenged and should be challenging themselves. At times this may give the appearance of a silent classroom with students deep in thought, however, some of my most successful lessons may have looked like an all-out riot. There have been times when the excitement of learning has been happening in my room that I have worried about an administrator walking by and misunderstanding our learning environment. Learning is chaotic, however, as teachers it is our job to ensure that the chaos of learning is a *controlled* form of chaos.

I have been a student of Kung Fu for many years. I love this system of martial arts for not only its proven combat techniques, but also for its gracefulness and fluidity. It wasn't until after several years of studying Kung Fu, however, that I realized that martial arts is a metaphor to life. There is more to this system than fighting and beautiful forms. Kung Fu is a philosophy and it is a way of life. Kung Fu can be applied to everything we do, and does not have to incorporate a single violent act.

While in class one evening, my instructor presented me with a scenario. I was being attacked by a much larger opponent who was advancing toward me. He grabbed my shoulders and began pushing me backward. My instructor then asked what I was going to do. Since I thought I was brave and tough, I began to push back on my opponent and demonstrated that I would also throw several kicks and elbows in hopes of wearing him down. But he was much stronger than I was, and after two minutes of defending myself, I found he had pushed me against the wall leaving me feeling completely exhausted. My tactics and defenses had failed and had that been a real situation, I would have taken a severe beating, or worse.

After I caught my breath, my instructor again had my opponent and I engage. He grabbed my shoulders and started to push me back. "STOP!" yelled my instructor. "Step back and to the side," he told me. At following his instructions, I took a step back and to the side. At doing so, my opponent that was pushing on me fell forward and struggled to regain his balance. "He is bigger and stronger than you. Why waste your own energy? Use his energy to redirect him where you want him to go," he told me. I can assure you, as a police officer I employed this technique regularly to help introduce violent suspects to the ground in order to stop their attacks. It works quite well.

So how can this apply to the classroom? Teachers are assaulted by their students every single day in every single class; not by fists and kicks, but by excuses, distractions, and arguments. I have learned from experience that engaging in every argument or debate would completely exhaust me, back me into a corner, and waste precious instruction time. My students outnumber me and their desire to avoid doing work is far stronger than my ability to constantly tell them to stop or stay on task. So what do I do? Instead of pushing back on them with a simple "no, stop," or "get back to work," I redirect the energy of their attack and place the burden back on them.

Redirection Examples:

Student: "I don't feel like doing this. Can I go to the bathroom?"

Teacher: "I'll tell you what, if you can get done the first five questions in the next 10 minutes, I'll write you a pass to the bathroom."

This compromise usually focuses the student to get some work done before leaving the room because their energy, or desire to go to the restroom, is redirected to first complete five questions.

Sometimes, however, the student will persist:

Student: "But it's an emergency!"

Teacher: "Then you better work fast."

*As you get to know your students, you will be able to better gauge if the student has a legitimate emergency or is simply trying to avoid doing work. Sometimes it may be better to just let them go.

Student: I think we should be able to have more free time during class.

Teacher: Why don't you write me a paragraph explaining your reasoning, and I'll consider it.

The energy from the student's desire for free time can be redirected to that of a class disruption to an educational writing assignment. If the student actually writes me a paragraph, I will compliment him on his argument and maybe reward him with an extra 5 minutes one day or give him extra credit for the assignment. I will also use it as a teachable moment to demonstrate to the class the respectful way to request something in comparison to the countless rude and inappropriate demands placed on teachers by students regularly, hence successfully redirecting and using the student's energy of avoidance for something positive.

Student: "This assignment is a waste of time. I'm not doing it and you can't make me."

Teacher: "You're right, I can't make you do it. So you have a choice to make: you can choose not to do the assignment and receive a 0, or you can give it a try and get the credit you deserve.

Student: "I'm not doing this."

Teacher: "Okay, that's your choice. But I'd hate for you to not get any credit today. Why don't you work on one of these other assignments?"

In the last example, the student continues to refuse to work on the assignment. As a teacher I can argue with the student and get into a power struggle that will most likely result in lost class time with the one student being sent to the office, in which case we both lose. I can ignore the student and he probably won't do the assignment and may then further disrupt other students. Again, we both lose. But if I present the student with one or two alternate assignments and allow the student to choose which one to work on, we both win. By giving students a choice, they still feel empowered. They are less likely to feel defensive by being *told* what to do in front of their friends, and are more likely to do something educational. In this scenario the student believes he avoided doing the assignment, but in reality he was simply redirected to another assignment.

When practicing classroom Kung Fu, it is more important for the student to decide to continue learning than it is for the student to be reminded that the teacher is in charge. As teachers, our main function is to teach. We have a specific set of information and knowledge we need to pass onto our students. If one student simply cannot read while sitting at his desk and needs to stand by the window in order to concentrate, why not let her? Our goal is to provide opportunities for learning, and learning does not always resemble neat, organized rows with hands raised in an orderly classroom. Students need to be free to explore their own learning styles, and so long as they are being respectful and not at risk of harming themselves or others, *let them!* They will learn more than you ever thought possible, and respect you more for it. Teaching, like Kung Fu, should be a fluid dance in an exchange of energy between teacher and student.

Classroom Kung Fu Principles

- *Do not engage a student in an argument – you will never win*
- *Redirect disruptive students to alternate seats or assignments to keep them engaged*
- *Provide students with choices, and inform them of the consequences of each choice*
- *Think outside the box – students do not need to be seated quietly in rows in order to learn!*

Strategy 6:
Plan B, C, and D…

As a teacher, it is safe to assume that things will rarely go as planned. *Something* always happens during instruction that demands we change or modify our lesson in order to keep the attention of our students. Sometimes students simply don't understand, sometimes they are too wound up, and sometimes we just create a terrible lesson! These challenges are a normal part of everyday teaching, and experienced teachers are experts at navigating these obstacles. But how do they do it?

In order to avoid a complete breakdown of structure and student engagement, every teacher should always have a *Plan B*. Plan B is an alternate lesson or a modified approach to a lesson that allows a teacher to easily transition when a lesson begins to fail without losing student engagement or instructional time.

With each lesson you plan, you should take into consideration the different learners in your class. Think about behaviors, learning disabilities, and learning styles. Then design multiple activities addressing the same learning goal. For example, if you are trying to teach students to identify the main idea in a story, does it matter if they all express that understanding in the same way? You may want every student to hand you a neatly written paragraph, but if you're strictly trying to assess their understanding of this concept, why not allow some students to write and some students to submit a picture or comic strip? You may initially assign your entire class to write a paragraph, but if you see some students struggling to complete the task, offer them the Plan B assignment to get them reengaged.

Unfortunately, there are occasions when an alternate assignment addressing the same goal or lesson is not enough. There are times when the entire lesson completely falls apart and the class has become completely disengaged. This can happen for any number of reasons, all of which can be equally stressful. In order to maintain structure in your classroom, however, teachers need to be able to completely drop a lesson or activity and start a new one quickly, as if it was what they were planning to do all along. But how does a teacher achieve this goal? Plan, plan, *plan!*

At any given time, in addition to my weekly lesson plans, I always have at least three Plan B lessons. I create these lessons in the beginning of the year, and sometimes I may go several weeks or even months before I have to use them. But on those days when I am trying to teach a concept and my students aren't engaging, I easily transition into my Plan B. I may even admit to the students that the current lesson isn't working and we will have to revisit it the next day. Students will often feel a sense of relief and view my "failure" as one of their victories, but also welcome the new lesson. As I mentioned in the Classroom Kung Fu chapter, teaching should be fluid, and we need to recognize when it's time to change direction.

A Plan B lesson does not have to be complicated. A simple newspaper or magazine article accompanied with comprehension questions or a writing assignment makes a great lesson and discussion. It can reengage students and you may even be able to get back into your original lesson once they are more focused.

In addition to having my Plan B, I also always have my Plans C and D ready. Plans C and D are alternate activities that do not require any work or instruction on my part that can be given to a student for any variety of reasons. For example, I often have one to two students who always finish their assignments ahead of everyone else. At times they may be finished everything 10 – 15 minutes before the rest of the class. With so much free time, I have witnessed even the most well-behaved students get into trouble and disrupt the rest of the class. In order to prepare for this scenario, I always have multiple activities for them to do once they complete their work. I establish a procedure so students know what to do and where to look when they are finished their assignments. For example, I require my students to keep a reading journal and log so many pages each week. If a student finishes all of their assignments and has nothing else to do, they know they are supposed to take out their book, read, and fill out their reading journal. In addition, I have several activities for them to complete for extra credit or amusement that don't give the appearance of extra work. (Word searches, crosswords, riddles, etc). My students know that once they finish their work they are to be reading, writing, or completing one of the other activities. This helps prevent the question of: "What do I do now?" It also frees the teacher from having to scramble to find something else for the student to work on at the last minute, in which case the student will most likely view it as busy work and not put much effort into it.

In my experience, however, I have also noticed that no matter how much planning I put into a lesson and my back-up plans, there are always scenarios I cannot prepare for. Sometimes something happens in the neighborhood or on the news that creates a strong emotional response among the students. There are times when strictly sticking to instruction are going to create more stress and anxiety, and the student's probably won't retain anything anyway. In those circumstances, I have found that sometimes a simple class discussion can go a long way. If you have built a good relationship with your students, they may want to talk to you and to each other about a particular incident. If I recognize that they are too upset to follow my lesson, I allow a discussion to take place but I am sure to set ground rules. Sometimes they only need a little bit of time, so I offer them a deal to have a discussion for 15 minutes as long as they then promise to complete the assignment I had prepared once we finish our conversation. In most cases, they appreciate the compromise and after some very deep emotional and meaningful discussions, they often get right to work. There are other circumstances, however, when the students are too upset to do anything beyond the discussion. There is nothing wrong with taking a class period to explore what is bothering them. I have taken advantage of multiple social concerns among my students and turned them into social and life skills lessons. As a teacher, these discussions have been some of my most rewarding experiences and I have found that in the days that follow my students are more eager to follow my instructions and complete whatever tasks I assign them.

Some Plan B (and C and D) Suggestions:

- *Provide students with an article to read. Have them answer questions, write a response, or have a discussion about the article.*

- *Writing assignments – I have several writing assignments I introduce throughout the year. Sometimes if I need a Plan B, I simply use one of my writing lessons.*

- *Grammar – My students work through a grammar workbook during the year. If a lesson isn't working, I will change direction and introduce a new grammar concept and have them work from their workbooks. There is no planning as the lessons are contained on the worksheets.*

- *Reading journals – My students should always have a book to read and when they finish their work they are to be reading or writing in their reading journals.*

- *Journaling – Students can write in their journals when they finish their work.*

- *Crosswords, Word Searches, and Riddles – these are fun activities that I don't always give out unless a student has completed all of their work to include their reading journal.*

The above-assignments are familiar to my students because they do them regularly. Many times, they don't even realize that I have abandoned a lesson and transitioned to my back-up plan. Regardless of which activities you prepare, the key is planning. As you learn to read your class, you will learn how best to navigate through your lessons and when to resort to your well prepared Plan B.

Strategy 7:
Unplug!

As I mentioned at the beginning of this guide, despite serving in the Army and working as a police officer, teaching has been the hardest thing I have ever done. My days are exhausting and emotionally draining because my students crave constant attention and engagement. My prep periods are spent grading, planning, writing IEPs, and meeting with students. During the school day, I rarely have any downtime and I even spend my lunch period in my classroom responding to emails or preparing another lesson. By the end of the day, I have barely enough strength to prepare dinner, and by the end of the school year my brain is usually so fried that I am incapable of logical thought.

If you find yourself about to lose your mind at any point during the year, whether it be the first week of school, right before Christmas Break, or in June, take refuge in knowing this happens to even the best of teachers. Our job is hard and we are constantly challenged in our day to day activities. I have had days where I was so angry that it took every ounce of restraint I had not to throw a kid out the window, and I have had days that were so emotionally trying that I found myself crying on the way home. Teaching is hard, and it can really take its toll on you. It is easy to become completely consumed by your job because our students often have some incredible needs that far exceed our own. But we must always remember to take care of ourselves, because if we fail to care for ourselves, we may become incapable of caring for others.

If we fail to take care of ourselves and become ill or too frustrated, then we severely limit our ability to help our students. As teachers it is easy to succumb to the demands of the job and spend nights and weekends grading papers, lesson planning, and writing IEPs. The paperwork seems never ending, and June often seems as if it will never arrive. But we need to make time for ourselves, otherwise we run the risk of being completely consumed by our jobs and burning out before mid-year.

I highly recommend setting aside 30 minutes to an hour every single day to do something completely unrelated to school. Take a walk, meditate, exercise, or watch your favorite TV show. I have learned that being able to completely forget about work for an hour each day allows me to recharge and come back fresh for the next challenge. As I mentioned above, I rarely get a break when I am at school, but I choose to operate this way so I don't have to bring work home with me. Once I'm done for the day I focus all of my attention on other things: family, home repairs, writing, and exercise.

It is important to develop a plan for yourself. Even if we are not focusing on school once we leave work, we can quickly become consumed by other distractions in life leaving us exhausted and drained for the following day's classes. I have found that in even the busiest of times at home, I can still set aside 30 minutes for myself in the morning to do Tai Chi. I started getting up earlier just to perform my exercises and I found myself forgetting about my stress and feeling refreshed at the beginning of my day. It makes a difference and on days that I am not able to do Tai Chi, I tend to carry a lot more frustration. Whatever it is that helps you relax, make the time to do it. Your students, and everyone else around you will benefit, including you.

Final Thoughts

As I was often told in the Army, "an ounce of prevention is worth a pound of cure." Take the time to prepare and implement these strategies. Work on preventing problems through your procedures instead of addressing them after they arise. Get to know your students, and you will grow to care about them. Avoid confrontation and remember the goal is to promote student learning, and not your authority. Always have a back-up plan, and remember to take care of yourself!

Additional Resources

I'd like to thank you for purchasing this guide. My goal was to provide my readers with a quick and easy to read guide with simple suggestions that would allow you to spend more time preparing and less time studying. However, if you enjoyed this guide or are looking for more information about teaching, then I highly recommend my book *Service, A Soldier's Journey: Counterintelligence, Law Enforcement, and the Violence of Urban Education*. It is a memoir of my experiences from Army Counterintelligence, to police work, to a violent Philadelphia special-education classroom.

The teaching experiences I detail in *Service* are a worst case scenario and I wrote the book in hopes of bringing about change for our students. If you are in education, especially if you are new to the field, this book is a *must* read. It will give you insight into just how bad things can get, and with that knowledge you can prepare yourself for the worst. As a soldier and cop, I have learned it is always best to prepare for the worst and hope for the best. Teaching is no different. Once you see just what my students and administrators put me through, I guarantee you will be much more prepared to handle just about any challenge you face throughout your teaching career.

In addition, as an expression of my gratitude for your purchase of this guide, I invite you to subscribe to our newsletter where you will receive FREE teaching resources and materials. It only takes a minute to register, but the resources you receive could save you hours in the classroom. For more information, please visit:

www.ServiceOfChange.com/Teachers

About the Author

Dennis Nappi II is a teacher, author, and advocate for education reform. In his free time, Dennis can be found gardening and hiking. Dennis is always looking for readers' feedback, experiences, and stories of positive change or success. If you'd like to contact Dennis, he can be reached at:

www.ServiceofChange.com

http://www.Facebook.com/ServiceOfChange

Service@ServiceOfChange.com

Twitter: @DennisNappiII

If you enjoyed this guide, please consider writing a review at your favorite online retailer to help other readers find this guide and support our movement toward education reform!

www.ingramcontent.com/pod-product-compliance
Lightning Source LLC
Chambersburg PA
CBHW061253040426
42444CB00010B/2376